To:

From:

Art Direction: Trinidad Vergara

Design: Renata Biernat

www.vergarariba.com

ISBN: 987-9338-62-6

Printed in Singapore

For the Love of My Life

Lidia María Riba

Art by Lola Frexas

V&R PUBLISHERS

My love, my lover, my companion...

my accomplice, my teammate,
my adviser.
Sometimes a son; sometimes, a father.
In some slightly irritating moments,
like my old headteacher.
In many others, my only ally.
The love of my life. You are all these things to me.
It took you barely an instant
to become some of them.
But the one I cherish most,
took a little longer:
today you are, without a single doubt,
my best friend.

I don't know if we fell in love at first sight.
But I do know that something magical
happened the first time I saw you.
And to this day, when I see you surrounded by people,
I know that there is no greater magic
than your piercing gaze seeking out mine.

Do you remember the beginning?
What a commotion,
what a complete change in our lives,
the risks we ran, the obstacles we had to overcome!
Whenever I look back,
I realize that this improbable, intense love,
must have had an overwhelming power,
strong enough to face anything.

If you weren't around...

I would go to bed early
and I would see my friends more often,
I'd go to the movies twice a week,
and stay up all night reading a novel,
I'd enjoy the city on Saturday afternoons
instead of driving out to the quiet country,
I wouldn't try quite as hard at the gym
and I'd turn up the volume on my favorite songs.

Now that I think about it... if you weren't
around, I would go to the end of the world
to find you.

You are my constant challenge:
the distant summit of that mountain
that I yearn to climb; the mysterious depth
that I just glimpse when I submerge;
the last corner to explore without a path to guide me.
With you it's impossible to think that
I've accomplished everything and stop,
finally, to rest.
That's why, loving you is –thankfully–
an endless adventure.

You have always believed in me...

even more than I've believed in myself.
But at times (who knows why!)
that infuriated me.
And yet, your conviction has
been my strongest support,
the source of energy to which I turn
when my strength starts to falter.
No one has ever believed in me the way you do,
and for that I will never be able
to thank you enough.

Meeting you – I'm not sure if I've ever told you this – strengthened my belief in God, by whatever name you call Him. Who else could have linked my destiny with yours? Who else would have chosen me – among all the people in the world – to be your companion? Who else could have imagined the incredible miracle of our finding each other?

I, who am such a big defender of the truth,
ask of you: don't tell me.
Don't tell me how many times,
in the middle of a fight,
you wanted to walk out forever.
Don't tell me how many times
I disappointed you when you
expected something special of me.
Don't tell me about that conversation
in which you found yourself envying the
unfettered freedom of a friend.
Don't tell me about that glance
you exchanged on the street...
Don't tell me and don't worry.
I won't tell you all my secrets either.

Now, we know each other...

and we can both guess almost exactly
what the other is thinking.
I know you won't tell me you were annoyed
that I wasn't there when you were looking for me.
You know how easily I take offense
when I sense you're being critical.
I know that in the early mornings
you prefer silence to conversation.
You know about my terrible distractions.
I know it's always been hard for you
to give presents.

But, when I least expect it,
when I think nothing can surprise me,
you show up with the most wonderful bouquet
of flowers. And I fall in love again,
because there is still so much to discover...

We celebrate many holidays
with family and friends.
But what an intimate and wonderful pleasure
to celebrate those secret anniversaries
that only we share.

One day, when you were away,
you called me full of enthusiasm:
you had discovered a very special place.
Describing it, you said
"It's paradise, we've got to come back together."
Then, we went on talking about other things.
Only later did I take time to relish that moment:
thank you, my love,
for wanting to take me to your paradise.

When you annoy me...

– always for the same reasons –
I stop for a minute and think:
this is the man who drove me crazy,
I suffered over him, and with him I also
discovered ecstasy…
Then, I surrender in a new moment
of blessed tolerance.

In our relationship there have been times
when we have fought over nothing and everything;
verbal battles that often ended with the loud
slamming of doors and threats never
carried out – thank God!
And later, passionate, all-consuming
reconciliations.
We have also grown together:we can sense
a warning light in a difficult conversation;
and our words become wiser, more sensitive.
But sometimes, just occasionally,
how satisfying to scowl and turn away,
only to fall into each other's arms again
vowing unconditional, eternal love…

Without you...

every act of my life would lose its meaning,
I would drift, without direction or destination,
because, while I don't hold you
responsible for my dreams,
you are the reason for every one
of them. Without you, what would I do
with the future, with each day ahead,
with my past and my memories?
You don't hear me but
I sometimes whisper softly:
please, stay by my side,
don't ever leave me.

If we nurture this love today,
deeper, more sure, more proven than
that first day's love,
there won't be…
difficulties we can't face,
hard times we can't endure,
storms we can't weather.
Nor will there be…
joys we don't share,
sorrows we can't overcome,
illnesses we don't help each other bear,
poverty we don't fight together,
wealth that could make us forget who we are.
And nothing will tear us apart.

Life by your side is like
a magnificent parade.
Sometimes I get the best seat,
I miss nothing and I enjoy
every detail: the music, the pageantry and the joy.
Other times, I can only glimpse what's going on,
I hear the chords from a distance
and I fight to get just a glimpse.
But I would always, always prefer to be part
of the parade than to walk alone
down the sad and empty street.

I can assure you
that I am an independent person, I have
searched and found my place in the world.
I enjoy every one of the things I do.
I have pursued and achieved many dreams
that have made me proud: work, relationships,
personal goals…
But none of them would mean the same
to me without your presence in my life,
which completes absolutely everything.

Share with me...

your dreams,
so that I can help you achieve them;
your triumphs,
because they will become mine too;
your worries,
so that your load is lighter;
your fears,
because they might fade if you say them out loud;
your disappointments and your rage,
I could fight for you against anyone;
your joys,
because what's yours is also mine;
your weariness,
so that I can lend you my strength;
your challenges,
so that I can help you prepare your weapons.
Share your journey with me.

We've always heard that the golden rule of relationships is to adapt, to get used to each other; that no one can change anyone else. But that's not true: you changed me and I changed you. (I think I changed you more, if you'll let me say so). It wasn't easy, but it was worth it: we made our miracle.

I love you in so many ways:
I love you joyously for the good times we share,
I love you patiently, faced with those habits of yours
that annoy me, I love you with hope
because there is still so much ahead of us,
I love you passionately and even a little innocently,
I love you with fear of losing you
and I love you with the confidence
of knowing you are mine.
I love you with this single condition:
that you love me too.

We have learned a few secrets...

to take our relationship forward:
taking what we say when we're in a bad mood
a little more light-heartedly
and what we feel when we're loving each other
a little more seriously.

Talking to each other,
expressing our feelings,
asking for more and expecting less,
but more than anything: knowing when to be quiet.
Despite everything people say about the
advantages of talking everything out,
occasionally, nothing is healthier
than silence.

Never forget the dream, that dream we shared
when everything seemed impossible
and unattainable.
Don't let it vanish amid the routine, the work,
or the pressure to conform.
Know that our vision, in love, is always behind the
mirror, blurred maybe, or just out of sight,
but waiting...

We have found the subtle harmony
of giving ourselves personal time and space,
to find ourselves in solitude
or to do whatever it is we like to do.
This may be the key that allows
us to enjoy the glory of each other's
company so much.

Sometimes I miss...

that stage of permanent uncertainty,
of watchfulness and anxiety,
because in our day to day lives we have
established certain routines which make
everything seem so calm.
But, night falls and in the intimacy that follows
we recognize each other again:
the passion has just been hiding.

Anyone who knows us
can see how different we are:
the books versus the sports;
the concerts versus the outdoors;
calm versus urgent;
sentimental versus practical.
But only we know that,
deep within our hearts,
we are identical:
we long for the same goals,
we dream of the same paradise,
and we are sure
that this love was destined to be
from the beginning of time.

Early one morning,
I was cleaning up our room as I thought about
the things I had to do that day.
Suddenly, as I was putting away some of your
clothes, the scent of you escaped from them,
strong and all-embracing.
I closed my eyes and inhaled.
Magically, the chores of the day disappeared.
We were two strangers again,
our eyes locked, they were playing our song
and nothing else mattered.
It all happened in an instant;
I closed the drawer and picked up the phone.
That night was unlike any other…

Our love...

was the excitement of the first kiss,
but it is also always having
your favorite salad dressing on the table;
it was waiting every minute to see if you would call,
but it is also running after you with those papers
that you forgot. Our love is the passion and the
timeless joy, but also the warmth of your hand
as we walk along; it was thinking about only you
all day, but it is also stopping
– even at my busiest – to ask how that meeting went.
Our love was the anxiety and the craziness
of those first moments,
but it is also the serenity of our present.
This love of yours and mine is our yesterday,
our today and the hope of our tomorrow.

This love, which has shown me the meaning
of fulfillment, will last forever,
because I cannot imagine it could end
in the brief span of my lifetime.
But, being human and limited,
I won't use the future tense to name it.
I do not own your future,
I don't even own mine.
I am only sure of one thing:
You are the love of my life,
and, today, I love you forever.